Make sure your memories will last a lifetime!

Journal dates:

_____

to

_____

> Dear children, servants, and friends, I trust to meet you all in heaven, both white and black.
> — Andrew Jackson

> Cursing is turned to blessing, injury into equity, suffering into glory, and the cross into rejoicing.
> — Martin Luther

> All of us have mortal bodies, composed of perishable matter, but the soul lives forever.
> — Flavius Josephus

Things we receive at God's hands come to us as truths from the minting house, though old in themselves, yet new to us. Old truths are always new to us if they come with the smell of Heaven upon them.

— John Bunyan

> No man is qualified for life, or any of its relations or duties, who fails of being benefited by the accumulating experience of the past.
>
> — Sebastian C. Adams

> As for the fear of danger that may come...my life is in the custody of Him whose glory I seek.
> — John Knox

> If then you will be a lily and a rose of Christ,
> know that you must be among thorns.
> — Martin Luther

> Let us rely on the goodness of our cause, and the aid of the Supreme Being, in whose hands victory is.
> — George Washington

> You can do more than pray, after you have prayed, but you cannot do more than pray until you have prayed.
>
> — John Bunyan

> Divine Providence has favored us with general health, with rich rewards in the fields of agriculture and in every branch of labor.
> — Andrew Jackson

> Family is the primary government whence all other government and dominion on earth take their origin.
> — Martin Luther

I will not repine...God is all sufficient.
— George Washington

> He who runs from God in the morning will scarcely find him the rest of the day.
> — John Bunyan

All the history of man, before the Flood, extant or known to us, is found in the first six chapters of Genesis.

— Sebastian C. Adams

> In whatsoever therefore you are deficient, seek the supply, prostrate before the Lord Jesus. He will teach you all things.
>
> — Martin Luther

> I bequeath my soul to God who gave it, hoping for a happy immortality through the atoning merits of our Lord Jesus Christ, the Saviour of the world.
> — Andrew Jackson

> Lord give us true pastors to thy church, that purity of doctrine may be continued, and restore peace to the nation, with goodly rulers.
>
> — John Knox

The whole power of the church lieth in the young, and if they are neglected, it will become like a garden that is neglected in the spring season.

— Martin Luther

> One leak will sink a ship: and one sin will destroy a sinner.
> — John Bunyan

> The kingdom of Christ is in the midst of his enemies.
>
> — Martin Luther

> See the wondrous works of Providence,
> and the uncertainty of human things!
> — George Washington

Our country has improved, and is flourishing beyond any former example in the history of nations.
— Andrew Jackson

> While Satan and his subjects rage, I will laugh and contemplate gardens, which are God's blessings, and enjoy them to his praise.
>
> — Martin Luther

> If in families obedience be not maintained, it is in vain to look for good government in a city, or province, or kingdom, or empire.
>
> — Martin Luther

> In prayer it is better to have a heart without words than words without a heart.
>
> — John Bunyan

We should consider, with a true Christian spirit,
that God alone is the judge of the hearts of men.
— George Washington

> Actuated by the sincere desire to do justice to every nation, and to preserve the blessings of peace, our intercourse with them has been conducted on the part of this government in the spirit of frankness.
> — Andrew Jackson

The cross of Christ is distributed throughout all the world, and to each one is always given his portion.
— Martin Luther

My only hope is in God.

— George Washington

Pray often— for prayer is a shield to the soul,
a sacrifice to God, and a scourge for Satan.
— John Bunyan

> Lord grant us a just and perfect hatred of sin.
> — John Knox

> The lessons contained in this invaluable legacy of Washington to his countrymen, should be cherished in the heart of every citizen to the latest generation.
> — Andrew Jackson

> I give thanks to God who has given me the victory.
>
> — John Knox

The believer is the alone man, by whom God showeth to the world the power of His grace.
— John Bunyan

> Whatever is not against the Scriptures is for the Scriptures, and the Scriptures for it.
> — Martin Luther

> I thank God that my life has been spent in a land of liberty, and that he has given me a heart to love my country.
>
> — Andrew Jackson

No child of God sins to that degree as to make himself incapable of forgiveness.

— John Bunyan

The supplicating tears of the women, and the moving petitions of the men, melt me with deadly sorrow.
— George Washington

> We called on God, and took him for our protector, defence, and only refuge.
> — John Knox

Through the mercy of our God, I have been enabled to conquer my fears.

— George Washington

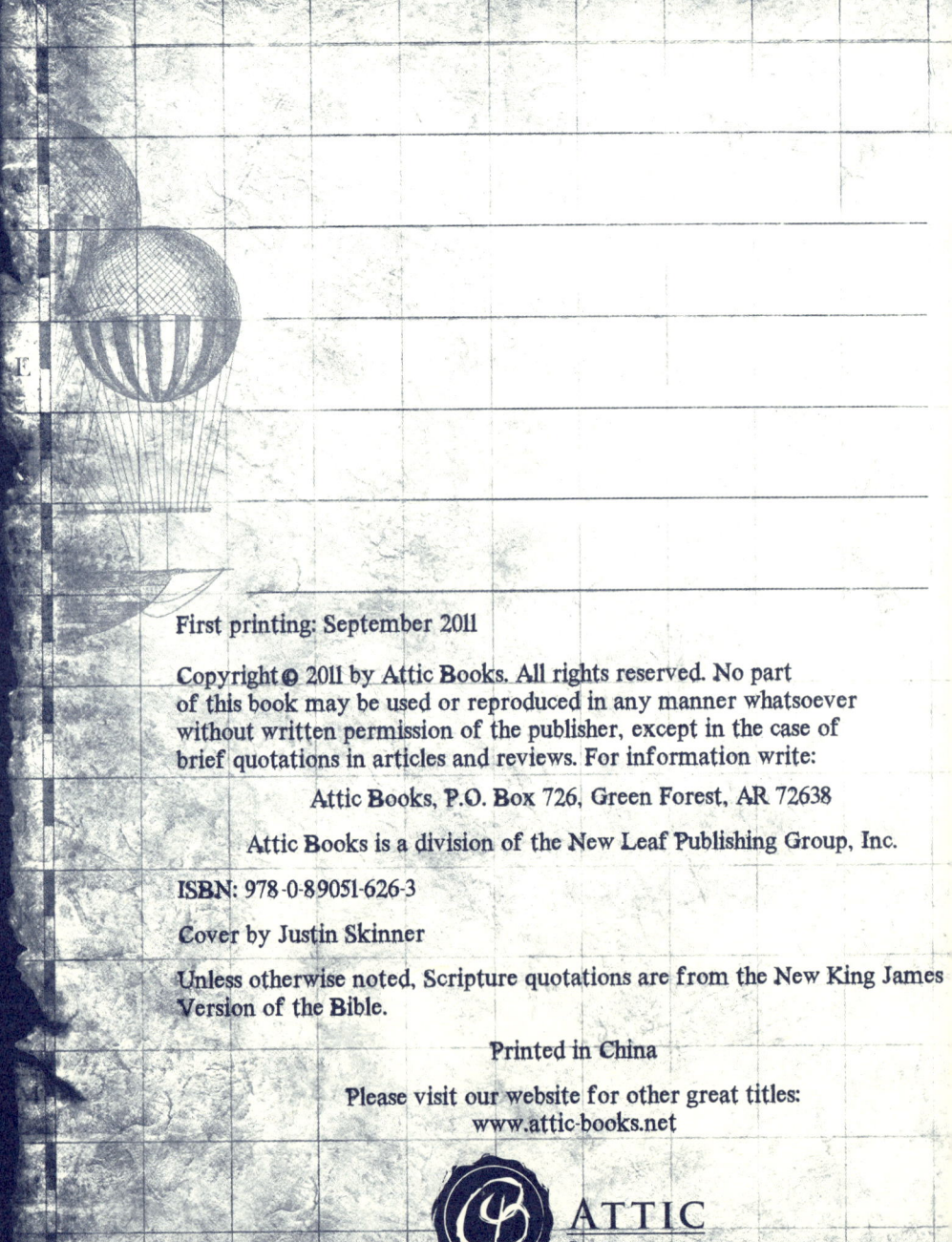

First printing: September 2011

Copyright © 2011 by Attic Books. All rights reserved. No part of this book may be used or reproduced in any manner whatsoever without written permission of the publisher, except in the case of brief quotations in articles and reviews. For information write:

Attic Books, P.O. Box 726, Green Forest, AR 72638

Attic Books is a division of the New Leaf Publishing Group, Inc.

ISBN: 978-0-89051-626-3

Cover by Justin Skinner

Unless otherwise noted, Scripture quotations are from the New King James Version of the Bible.

Printed in China

Please visit our website for other great titles:
www.attic-books.net

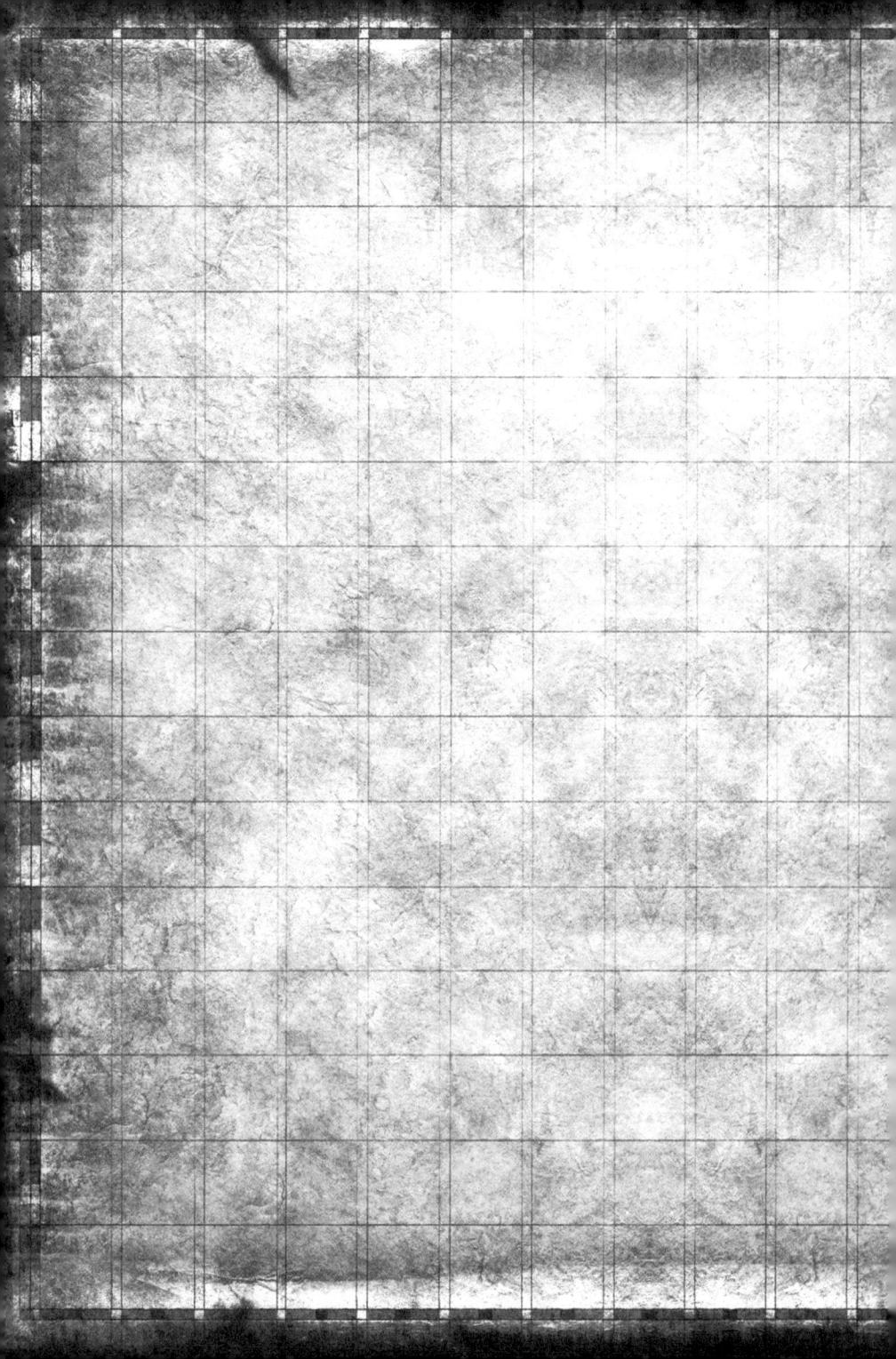